The Weather
CLOUDS

Terry Jennings

Chrysalis Children's Books

First published in the UK in 2004 by
Chrysalis Children's Books
An imprint of Chrysalis Group PLC
The Chrysalis Building, Bramley Road, London W10 6SP

ISBN 1 84458 072 5

British Library Cataloguing in Publication Data
for this book is available from the British Library.

Produced by Bender Richardson White

Editorial Manager: Joyce Bentley
Project Editors: Lionel Bender and Clare Lewis
Designer: Ben White
Production: Kim Richardson
Picture Researcher: Cathy Stastny
Cover Make-up: Mike Pilley, Radius

Printed in China

10 9 8 7 6 5 4 3 2 1

Words in **bold** can be found in New words on page 31.

Contents

Up in the sky

Sometimes the sun shines
in a clear, blue sky.
Sometimes there are white
clouds in the sky.

On **dull** days, clouds
cover all of the sky.

What are clouds?

Most clouds are made of
tiny drops of water.

You can see these water drops when **rain** collects on cobwebs or on a window.

Water to clouds

The sun's heat changes the water in ponds, rivers, seas and other wet places to invisible steam.

The steam rises, cools down
and changes back to tiny drops
of water. This makes a cloud.

Falling water

Later, the water in a cloud falls back to the ground again. It falls as rain or, on cold days, as **hail** or **snow**.

Rivers carry the water back
into lakes or the sea.

Flat clouds

There are different kinds of clouds. Flat clouds are called **stratus clouds**.

They are often grey and dull.
They hide the sun, and they
often bring rain.

Wispy clouds

Thin wispy clouds are known as **cirrus clouds**. They are high in the sky where it is very cold.

Cirrus clouds tell us that the weather is about to change.

Fluffy clouds

Big, fluffy clouds are called **cumulus clouds**. You often see them on warm, sunny days.

Sometimes cumulus clouds bring a shower of rain. Sometimes they grow into dark thunderclouds.

Thunderclouds

The largest clouds of all make **thunder**. Thunderclouds grow bigger and bigger.

Soon they produce rain or tiny pieces of **ice** called hail. These look like little white stones.

Lightning

Electric energy builds up in thunderclouds. This causes huge flashes of **lightning**.

When lightning flashes, it heats the air. It makes the crashing noise we call thunder.

Mist

Mist is a blanket of thin clouds near the ground. You can see through these clouds.

Mist often forms near rivers and seashores on warm days.

Fog

In cool, damp weather **fog** often forms near the ground. Fog is a thick cloud made of large drops of water.

On the roads, fog makes it difficult for drivers to see where they are going.

Making clouds

Some clouds are made by steam or smoke coming from factories. Big chimneys carry them into the air.

Explosions such as rockets firing or fireworks make clouds of smoke.

Above the clouds

Even when the clouds hide the sun, the sun is still shining.

From space, you can see
white swirls of clouds all
over the earth. They are lit
by the sun.

Quiz

1 What are most clouds made of?

2 What does the sun's heat change water into?

3 What do we call flat, dull grey clouds?

4 What do we call the pieces of ice which sometimes come from a thundercloud?

5 What do we call a thick cloud that is near the ground?

6 Which are the largest clouds?

7 What are the clouds from factories made of?

8 Does the sun shine above the clouds?

The answers are all in this book!

New words

cirrus cloud a wispy cloud high in the sky.

cloud a mass of tiny water drops, smoke or dust floating in the air.

cumulus cloud a big, fluffy cloud that looks like cotton wool.

dull not bright, gloomy.

fog a thick cloud near the ground.

hail pieces of ice that fall from the sky; they look like little stones.

ice frozen water.

lightning a flash of light in the sky during a thunderstorm.

mist a cloud of very small water drops floating in the air near to the ground.

rain drops of water that fall from the sky.

snow soft pieces of ice falling from the sky as white flakes.

steam a gas produced by heating water, such as boiling a kettle.

stratus cloud a low, flat cloud that covers the sky.

thunder the loud crash that follows lightning in a thunderstorm.

Index